seeking **religion**

The **Hindu** Experience

Jan Thompson

Foundation

<u>Hodder & Stoughton</u>

A MEMBER OF THE HODDER HEADLINE GROUP

Acknowledgements

Dedicated to:
Paul Gateshill,
a friend and colleague

Notes:

> CE = Common Era
>
> BCE = Before the Common Era
>
> CE corresponds to AD, and BCE corresponds to BC. The years are the same, but CE and BCE can be used by anyone, regardless of their religion. (AD and BC are Christian: AD stands for Anno Domini – in the Year of our Lord i.e Jesus Christ; BC stands for Before Christ.)

Key words are explained in the glossary on page 63.

Orders: please contact Bookpoint Ltd, 130 Milton Park, Abingdon, Oxon OX14 4SB. Telephone: (44) 01235 827720, Fax: (44) 01235 400454. Lines are open from 9.00–6.00, Monday to Saturday, with a 24 hour message answering service. You can also order through our website www.hodderheadline.co.uk

British Library Cataloguing in Publication Data
A catalogue record for this title is available from The British Library

ISBN 0 340 77581 5

First published 1992
Second edition 2000
Impression number   10 9 8 7 6 5 4
Year   2005   2004   2003

Copyright © 2000 Jan Thompson, Liz Aylett and Kevin O'Donnell

Cover photo from Philip Emmett.
All illustrations supplied by Daedalus, with special thanks to John McIntyre.
Typeset by Wearset, Boldon, Tyne and Wear.
Printed in Italy for Hodder & Stoughton Educational, a division of Hodder Headline
338 Euston Road, London NW1 3BH.

The publishers would like to thank the following for permission to reproduce copyright photographs in this book:

Asha Bains: p38; CIRCA Photo Library: pp23 (William Holtby), 45, 53 (John Smith); Corbis/Hulton Deutsch: pp57r, 60; Philip Emmett: pp6, 8r 10, 17, 30, 31, 32, 39, 48, 54, 55, 57l, 61, 62; Hodder & Stoughton Library: p9; Hulton Getty Picture Collection Ltd: p59; ISKCON Educational Services: pp11, 16r, 56; Christine Osborne/MEP: pp5, 12, 15, 16l, 18 21, 28, 35, 40, 41, 42, 49, 51, 58r; David Rose: pp19, 26, 29, 36, 37, 43, 44, 50; Science Photo Library: p8l.

The publishers would like to thank the following for permission to reproduce material in this volume:

The Ramakrishna Vedanta Centre for the extract from *Essentials of Hinduism*; The Open University for extracts from *Man's Religious Quest*; Michael Joseph Ltd for the extracts from *Seasons of Splendour* by Madhur Jaffrey; India Book House Limited for the illustration from *Tales of Durga*, which is reproduced with permission from Amar Chitra Katha © India Book House Limited.

Minor adaptations have been made to some quotations to render them more accessible to the readership.

Every effort has been made to trace and acknowledge ownership of copyright. The publishers will be glad to make suitable arrangements with any copyright holders whom it has not been possible to contact.

Contents

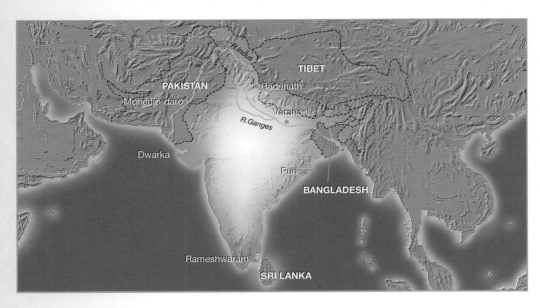

◄ *This is a map of India. It is where Hinduism started. It is where most Hindus still live*

4

TASK

With a partner, see how many Indian things you can think of. Do you know anything about Indian food, music, dress or religion? Use these ideas to make a list of all the things you know about India.

This book is about Hinduism. This is a religion. It comes from India. As you learn about Hinduism, you will find out that it is a very Indian religion.

If you are lucky enough to visit a Hindu temple, you will see the bright colours which Indian people love. There will be Indian music and Indian food.

India is a very big country. It is over 14 times bigger than Britain. People in different areas live in different ways. They even speak different languages. So as Hinduism spread through India, it grew in different ways.

We all have different sides to our characters. Your teacher may not see the same side of you as your parents do! Hindus believe that God has many sides to his character. They show this by having many different pictures and statues of gods and goddesses. Hindus appear to worship more than one God. But Hinduism teaches that these are different ways to think about God.

The following words are from a very old Hindu holy book. They show that Hinduism teaches that there is really only one God.

God is One, but wise men call Him by different names.

Rig Veda 1.164.46

People cannot live without water. In a hot, dry country like India, the rivers are very important. Hinduism first grew up around the River Indus. This is where the name 'Hinduism' comes from. Most of the River Indus is now in modern Pakistan. This was part of India until the middle of the 20th century. Try to find the river on the map.

Hinduism is the oldest of the religions that exist today. There were people living near the River Indus about 5000 years ago. Remains of their cities have been dug up. Some things that Hindus do today come from that time. For example, they worshipped both gods and goddesses.

About 3500 years ago a people called the Aryans invaded India from the North. These people brought new religious ideas. For example, they worshipped around a fire. They also had different gods, like Indra the god of thunder. This is what they said about him:

> Men do not win without him. They call on him for help when fighting ... He is Indra.

Hinduism has grown and changed over thousands of years. Therefore there are many differences in Hinduism. There are different details in their stories. There are different festivals and ways of worship. And there are many names for God.

Key words

Hinduism
Hindus
Hindu
religion
temple

▶ Some of the remains of an old ruined city by the River Indus

Fire and water were very important to the people who lived by the River Indus 5000 years ago. They are still used in Hinduism today. In this photo of Hindu worship, you can see a water jug on the floor, and a fire.

Water is very important in a hot country like India. So Hindus use water in their worship of God.

Fire reminds them of God's power.

▲ *Hindus today still use fire in their worship*

1 Make up a sentence for each of the words in the word box.
Show that you understand each word and can use it properly.

2 Write the answers to these questions in full sentences:
a) In which country do we find most Hindus?
b) Which river gave its name to Hinduism?
c) How old is Hinduism?

FIRE

3 Your teacher may like to darken the room and light a candle. Sit quietly looking at it for at least a minute. Afterwards, think how you felt. You may like to talk about it. Why does a flame hold our attention?

WATER

4 Talk about a time when you were very thirsty, and thankful for a drink of water.

5 Water is used in many religions. Can you think of another example? (Clue: How is water used with babies in some Churches?)

This is the main badge of Hinduism. It is written in a very old Indian language, called Sanskrit. It says Aum, or A-U-M. **Aum is used in Hinduism to stand for God who is called Brahman.**

'Guru' is the Indian word for 'teacher'. Gurus are wise and holy men who have passed on their wisdom to others. Most Hindus today follow a guru. We also know what some of the earliest Hindu gurus said, over 2500 years ago.

▲ *The Aum symbol*

Key words

Aum
symbol
Sanskrit
guru
Brahman

7

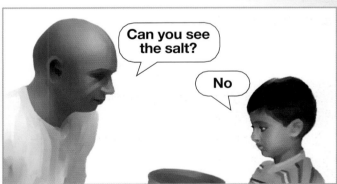

Sometimes the holy men spoke of Brahman as a person. Sometimes they spoke of Brahman as impersonal, like a power or force.

Some Hindus believe that the different gods and goddesses are there to help them worship Brahman. It is easier to worship a person than an 'it'.

Others believe that God really is a person, and that he wants people to love him above all others.

Hinduism lets people think of God in different ways: as a vast power and also as a loving person.

▲ *A father and child at a Hindu temple*

▲ *Vast endless space*

1 Copy the Aum symbol and label it.

2 Make up a sentence for each of the words in the word box. Show that you understand each word and can use it properly.

3 Look at the TWO photos on this page. What TWO ideas do they suggest about God?

4 Design something to show your own idea of God for a classroom display. What do you want it to say? Will it suggest greatness and power? Or will it show something loving, that makes you feel safe?

Hindus made up the game of Snakes and Ladders that we now play in Europe. Snakes and Ladders is a game of ups and downs, just like life. But in this game, you move up or down because of a chance throw of a dice. Is life like this? Hindus believe that what happens in life is *not* by accident. They think that we bring it upon ourselves by our past actions.

This Hindu belief is called karma. They believe that karma works like a scientific law. **Karma is the law of action and reaction. That means that whatever you do has its results.** Good actions earn good karma and bring good results. Bad actions earn bad karma and bring bad results.

It is easy to understand how different actions bring different results. Look at the cartoon below:

- If someone shares, this makes people like them. They will trust them and speak well of them to others.
- But if someone is nasty, people will dislike them. They won't want to be friends with them and will speak badly of them to others.

Sometimes we can see the results of our actions straight away. Sometimes the results of our actions come many years later.

▲ *Snakes and Ladders*

▲ *Our actions affect our lives, and those around us*

TASK

Talk about these questions with a partner:

- Do you think our actions always have results? Give some examples.
- Can you think of any actions which might have results years later?
- Do you think anything happens by chance? Choose one of the situations you have talked about. Prepare a role-play on it to act to the rest of the class. You should be able to explain why you chose it.

Many other things have come to Europe from India. Look at the cartoons below.

- The Hindus knew that the earth was round. They knew this 1000 years before the people of Europe.
- Hindus made up our number system. It passed from India to Arabia, and the Arabs took it to Europe.
- Do you know what the woman is doing in the photo? Find out how cotton is spun.

▲ *Many of our ideas depend upon knowledge from ancient India*

▲ *Ways of making cotton cloth come from India*

Key word

karma

1 Design a karma board-game with snakes and ladders on it. Draw a grid of squares (10 × 10). On some of the squares, write examples of good or bad deeds. If you land on a good action, you should move forward or up a ladder. If you land on a bad action, you should go backwards or down a snake.

There are many holy books in Hinduism. A person could not read them all in a lifetime! Some are so difficult that only the priests and teachers can read them. Others are stories that everyone can enjoy.

The oldest holy books are called Vedas, which means 'knowledge'. Hindus believe the Vedas came from God and have everything a person needs to know about the world. They are written in Sanskrit, the old Hindu language.

> Sanskrit is a very difficult language. I did a degree in Sanskrit, but when our priest speaks Sanskrit I can't understand it! So he speaks Sanskrit in the temple and then he explains it in Hindi and English.

▼ A Hindu holy book – for English readers

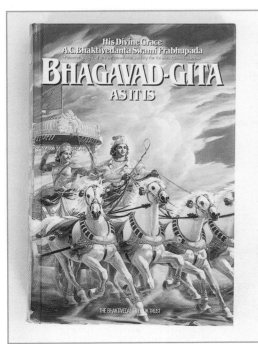

The Vedas include prayers and songs for the priests. They tell them how to worship. At the end of the Vedas are the teachings of wise men. They went off into the forests with their pupils and tried to answer all the difficult questions about life.

TASK

- Where would you go if you wanted to be quiet to think about things?
- Think of a question about life that you would like to ask a wise person.

Key words

Vedas	**Vishnu**
Gita	**Krishna**

▼ *The prayer below is in Sanskrit and English. Ask your teacher to read the first part of it out loud. This is what Sanskrit sounds like*

PRAYER

ASATO MAA SAD GAMAYAA
TAMASO MA AJYOTIR GAMAYAA
MRITYORMA AMRITAM GAMAYAA

O God, lead us from untruth to truth, Lead us from darkness to light, and lead us from death to life.

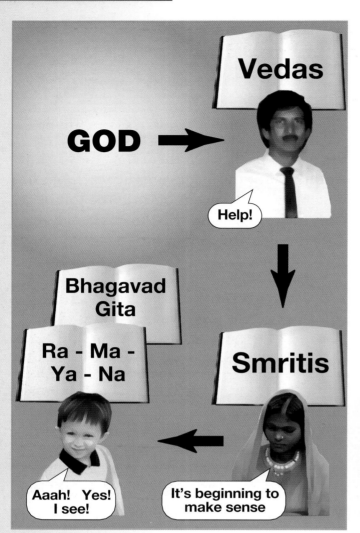

GOD → **Vedas**

Help!

Bhagavad Gita

Ra - Ma - Ya - Na

Smritis

Aaah! Yes! I see!

It's beginning to make sense

▲ *Hindu holy books*

TASK

- What do we look up in dictionaries? These are books that help us to understand other books.
- What famous stories do you know? They could be fairy-tales.

Most Hindus cannot read the Vedas in Sanskrit. Even when they are translated, they are very difficult to understand.

So Hindu teachers wrote the smritis to try to explain the Vedas. But these are still very old books, written about 2500 years ago. They too need explaining!

So there are many other books in Hinduism for ordinary people. They use stories to help Hindus understand their religion.

Since I've been here, I haven't heard anybody reading the Vedas. Mostly the priest teaches about *Bhagavad Gita* and *Ramayana*. He reads Sanskrit first and then he explains in Hindi.

One well-loved story book is called the *Bhagavad Gita* (or just *Gita*). It means 'Song of the Lord'. Another is the *Ramayana*, about Prince Rama. Hindus believe that the god Vishnu came to earth as Rama.

▲ *Hindus believe that the god Vishnu also came to earth as Lord Krishna*

One very old Hindu book is a poem with 110,000 verses! It tells the history of India long ago. It is about a battle between good and evil. This poem is called the *Mahabharata*.

The eldest brother of the Kurus was blind, and so he could not become king. His brother, Pandu, became king, instead.

Pandu wanted to live as a holy man, and so he gave the kingdom to his brother.

The king took Pandu's five sons into his palace and treated them as his own. His own sons were jealous, and planned to kill them. They escaped to the forest, led by Prince Arjuna.

A great battle started that lasted for 18 days. At last, the sons of Pandu won and ruled wisely.

▲ *The story of the* Mahabharata

A small part of this vast history has become the most loved of all Hindu holy books. This is the *Gita*. It tells the story of 2 related families that went to war over who should be the next king.

As they got ready for battle, Prince Arjuna worried about fighting his own relatives. He asked his chariot driver for advice. This driver was in fact Lord Krishna! He told Arjuna that he was a soldier and that it was his duty to fight. He told him not to worry about killing or being killed. He said that only the body dies and that the real person inside that body lives on. So Arjuna went into battle, and won.

The *Gita* sums up the main beliefs of Hinduism. It teaches that people will only be happy if they do what they are meant to do in life. It also teaches people to love God and worship him.

This is what the great Indian leader Gandhi said about the *Gita*:

> When I do not know what to do ... and I see no hope, I turn to the *Gita* and find a verse to comfort me. I immediately begin to smile in the middle of sorrow.

▼ *Krishna teaches Arjuna and showed himself as God*

Prince Arjuna faced members of his family in battle. He did not want to fight them, but they had done wrong and cheated many people.

I have no heart for this... my own relatives face me...

You know it is your duty to punish wrongdoing, and to restore justice.

Krishna explained that only the bodies of the soldiers could be killed. Their souls would live on, and be reborn.

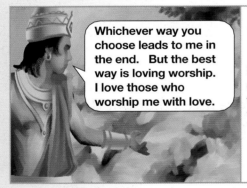

Whichever way you choose leads to me in the end. But the best way is loving worship. I love those who worship me with love.

Krishna explained that there are many ways to God.

Krishna revealed his glory to Arjuna, as an appearance of God on Earth.

1 Write a sentence which includes both the words Vedas and Sanskrit.

2 Read what Gandhi wrote about the *Gita*. What effect did it have on him?

3 Write or talk about a time when something has cheered you up.

4 Make up a story together in class about a struggle between good and evil. Decide if you want to set it in the past, today or future. Choose the main characters (the 'goodies' and 'baddies'). Work out the events in the story. Each of you should design a cover for the story.

Hindus do not have to believe exactly the same as each other. It will depend on their background and education or what they have decided for themselves. But there are some things which nearly all Hindus believe.

There is one God (Brahman)

Hindus believe that there is one God. They think of God in many ways and call him by many names.

Hindus believe that God is everywhere and in everything. He is like the salt in salt water. You cannot see the salt, but it is in every part of the water. Gandhi said this:

> While everything around me is always changing, always dying, there is a living power that does not change, that holds everything together. That power or spirit is God.

And this is what a Hindu holy book says about God:

> You are woman. You are man.
> You are the dark-blue bee
> and the green parrot with the red eyes.
> The lightning is your child.
> You are the seasons of the year
> and the sea.
> You are part of everything.
> You are everywhere.

We each have a soul (Atman)

Hindus believe that there is a part of God in everyone. This is called their soul (or atman).

> - The body is like a car and your soul drives around in it.
> - The body is just like a bag. It's full of blood and bones. It's not as important as the soul.

▲ *The Hindu greeting*

When Hindus meet, they put their hands together, bow their heads and say 'Namaste' (pronounced 'Na-mass-tay'). This means 'I bow to you with respect.' This is how they show their belief that God lives in everyone. They are bowing to God inside you. Would you treat people differently if you thought that God was in them? This is how a Hindu holy book puts it:

> A wife loves her husband not for his own sake . . . but because the Atman lives in him . . . Children are loved not for their own sake, but because the Atman lives in them . . .

Hindus believe that our conscience is the part of us that responds to God. It reminds us that God is deep within us, as our soul.

The photo below shows 3 generations: a child, his parents and his grandmother. It reminds us that we change as we grow older. You looked different as a child, and you will change as you grow older. We also think differently as we go through life. We don't expect an adult to think and behave like a child.

So where is the real you? Who is the real person within?

In a way we are always changing. But it is the same person within us doing the changing. Think about this story:

A man once lent his friend £20. One day, they met in a crowd. The man remembered his £20.
'What do you mean?' asked his friend.
'I'm not the same person as I was then. I'm different!'
How would you have felt if it had been your money?

We can point to different parts of our bodies. But can we point to ourselves? The photo below shows some children trying to do just that!

▲ *Three generations of a Hindu family in south London*

▲ *A Hindu priest with school children*

1 Draw an outline of a body and put the title: 'The soul'. Inside the body, draw things that make you 'you' (eg anything that is personal or special to you).

2 a) Collect some photos of yourself as you have grown up. You look very different now from when you were a baby. Yet you are the same person.

b) Invent a drama of yourself as you are now, meeting with yourself when you were a child at primary school. What would you say to each other?

Reincarnation (and Karma)

Hindus believe that when you die your soul is reborn on earth in a new body. This is called reincarnation.

You have already read about karma in Chapter 3. It is the belief that everything we do affects us in some way. Hindus believe that this goes on from one life to the next. The sort of person you become in this life will affect your rebirth. This is explained in the source below. It is from one of the Hindu holy books.

Each rebirth gives the soul a chance to improve and to be born into a better life next time round.

Non-violence (Ahimsa)

Many Hindus believe in non-violence. This means that they try not to harm any living thing. One Hindu who believed in non-violence was Gandhi. He was a great Indian leader in the first half of the 20th century. He wasn't afraid to speak out against things that were wrong in society. But he refused to use violence. He led peace marches against the government. But he would not let the people fight, even to defend themselves. He won the argument, and he is still loved by the Indian people today.

> Those who behave well in this life will have a good rebirth. But those who do wrong will have a bad rebirth. They will be reborn as a dog or as a pig.
>
> People make their next lives by what they think and do in this life. A caterpillar puts its front feet firmly on the next leaf before stepping off the last leaf. In the same way, each soul makes its next life before leaving this one.

Key words

soul
conscience
reincarnation
non-violence

▲ *A peaceful protest in India*

1 Do you think there is any truth in the Hindu belief in reincarnation? Try to give reasons for what you think.

2 What do you think these people ought to come back as:
   a) a doctor   **b)** a murderer
   c) a charity worker   **d)** a thief?

Respect for nature

Most people in India still live in villages in the countryside. They live close to nature and depend upon it. They grow crops and keep animals. Their houses are small and they spend a lot of time out of doors. They often cook, eat and wash out in the open.

Hinduism teaches them to respect nature. This is because they believe that everything comes from God, so they should be thankful for it and care for the earth. They also believe that there is a part of God, a soul, in every living thing. Therefore they should respect people, animals and even plants.

The photo below shows a Hindu shrine at a special tree. Local Hindus come here to worship God. Hindus see God in every part of nature, and shrines can be found at trees, caves and springs of water.

Hindus show great respect for cows. They regard them as sacred or holy. This is because:

- the cow is a gentle animal
- it does not kill to eat
- it is a mother
- it gives milk for food.

The cow teaches Hindus about God. They believe that God is gentle and kind. They believe that God gives life and food. So Hindus love cows and do not harm them. They let them walk the streets in India, and they feed them their scraps.

▲ *A Hindu tree shrine*

The cow provides milk.

This gives butter, ghee, yogurt, cream and cheese.

Ghee is used for offerings.

Oxen pull carts and ploughs.

They are also used for milling and irrigation.

Dried dung is used for walls, floors and for fuel and fertiliser.

▲ *Cows and bulls are very useful. Hindus do not kill them for meat*

Many Hindus are vegetarian. They do not want to kill an animal for food. They believe that God is in all life. And they believe in non-violence towards animals. So they make meals from rice, bread, milk, vegetables, pulses (like beans and lentils) and fruit.

When Hindus cook food, they offer some to God for him to bless it. Then they mix some of this back into the rest of the food so that everyone can share in God's blessing.

▲ *Offering food at a home shrine in England*

---

1 Take a page in your book and divide it in half across the middle. In both halves, draw the outline of a tree with 4 very large leaves on it.
a) In the top tree, write inside each leaf a reason why Hindus respect nature.
b) On the bottom tree, write inside each leaf your own feelings about trees.

2 a) If you live in a large town or city, talk about how easy it would be to be cut off from nature. (eg can you see the stars at night?).
b) If you live in the country, talk about things from nature which you can see.
3 Put the title 'The sacred cow'. Draw an outline of a cow. Write inside all the reasons why cows are sacred for Hindus .

Caste and Dharma

TASK

Think together in class about our own society.

Talk about the following questions:

- Do we have a class system?
- Are some people well treated just because of their family backgrounds?
- Are some people badly treated for no fault of their own?

● **The caste system**

There is a very old Hindu idea that people are divided into groups by birth. The 4 main classes are shown in the pictures below. Within each class there are lots of smaller groups called castes. There is a different caste for the different jobs that people do. At one time Hindus could only do the work of the caste that they were born into.

This Hindu idea is called the caste system.

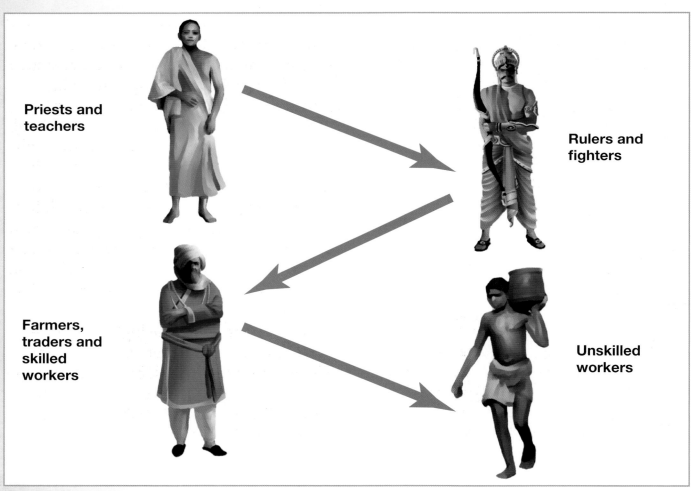

Priests and teachers

Rulers and fighters

Farmers, traders and skilled workers

Unskilled workers

▲ *The 4 main groups, in order of importance*

There is an important reason for the caste system. Hindus believe that everyone has a special duty. This duty is called dharma. It means holy law. Hindus believe it is their duty to do the work of their caste. Skills have been passed down through families, and they have a duty to use those skills. This is their dharma.

▲ *Untouchables do the worst jobs*

TASK
- Talk about the career you would like to have when you leave school.
- Are there any advantages in doing the same work as your parents?
- Imagine that you *had* to follow the same career as your parents, but you felt you had different talents. Work out a role-play in which you talk to your parents. What would you say to them? What might they say to you?

There is another group of people who do not belong to any caste. They are sometimes called 'Untouchables'. They do all the nasty jobs like cleaning the toilets and roads and getting rid of dead animals.

Until about 50 years ago, Untouchables could mix freely only with each other. They were banned from many public places. They could not go to school. They could not even get water from a public well. They could only travel by train if there was a place set aside for them.

> Only people from our own caste can come here and eat with us off our plates. There would never be any question of us eating with Untouchables. When we give food to our servant, he either eats off his own plate or we give him a clay plate which is then tossed away.

21

Not all Hindus believe in the caste system. Some believe that there was an earlier system in Hinduism which let people move into higher groups if they were good enough.

An old story supports this idea. It tells of a young man who went to study with a holy man. The holy man wanted to know who his father was. He said he would have to ask his mother. His mother said she didn't know because she had been with many men. He went back and told the holy man that he did not know who his father was. Then the holy man said: 'I say you are a Brahmin, for your soul is good!'

The Brahmins were the highest of the 4 Indian groups. They were the priests and religious teachers. (Look back at the picture chart on the page opposite.) (NB Do not confuse 'Brahmin' with 'Brahman' which is the name for God.)

Gandhi was a great leader who changed many things in India. (You can read more about him in Chapter 16.) Although he was born into a high caste, he spoke out for the Untouchables. He called them Children of God. He set up a community where everyone lived as equals. They all shared the work. Gandhi even took his turn at cleaning the toilets.

Many of Gandhi's ideas came from the Hindu holy book called the *Gita*. The passage below seems to say the same as the story on page 21. In that story, the boy's good soul was more important than his birth. The *Gita* also teaches that a person's character is more important than the class they were born into. This passage lists the things that make a good Brahmin.

The Untouchables are the Children of God.

▲ *Gandhi*

> These are the things that make a good Brahmin:
> not fighting; not losing his temper; being strict with himself; having pure thoughts; being patient with other people; telling the truth; wanting to learn things; thinking about things and being religious.
>
> *Ideas from the* Gita *18:42*

The modern country of India was formed in 1947. Its new government made it illegal to treat people differently because of their caste. The Untouchables are now called 'Dalits' which means 'the oppressed class.' Some have gone to university and now have good jobs. One Indian president was a dalit! Things have changed more quickly in the towns and cities than in the villages. It is easier to be educated in the cities and there are new jobs to do. Village life is much more difficult to change. People know each other's families and keep their old jobs.

Even where the caste system is not so strong, most Hindus still want to marry someone from their own caste.

22

1 Make up a sentence for each of the words in the word box. Show that you understand each word and can use it properly.

2 Put the title 'The caste system'. Draw and label the 4 main groups.

3 a) What were Hindus called who did not belong to these 4 groups?
   b) What kind of jobs did they do?
   c) Why do you think Gandhi called them Children of God?

4 Make up your own story to show that a person's character is more important than their birth.

◄ *We often have to work hard to achieve our goals*

We all have things we want to do in life. These are our goals. In football, we want to score and win. In the high jump, we want to jump higher. In exams, we study to pass. There are many goals like this. But what are the most important goals in life?

I want to be...   I want to do...

▲ *What do we really want out of life?*

The biggest goal for all Hindus is the same. **They want to be free. Hindus want to escape from rebirth when they die. They want their souls to return to God. They call this escape 'moksha'.**

The way to do this is to make sure that each rebirth takes the soul to a better life. Think of it like going up a league table. A good life is like a win and promotion. A bad life is like a defeat, and the soul goes down the league table.

Each promotion means that the soul understands a little more about the world and about God. The highest rebirth is that of a priest. They have the best chance to escape from rebirth.

Remember that karma is the belief that everything we do affects us in some way.

This belief explains why one person is good and another bad ... We must not blame our parents. It is our karma that results in joy or sorrow, pleasure or pain. Again and again we are reborn on this earth to learn more lessons.

23

▲ *Some of the things people want from life*

We can have many goals in life. But some of them do not last. The latest fashions and a new car do not last for ever.

Only spiritual things last for ever. This is why Hinduism teaches people to ignore worldly pleasures. Hindus are told to use their life to get closer to God. Then they should have a good rebirth. And maybe, they will escape for ever from the endless round of rebirths. This is what 2 Hindu writers say about this:

- What I want to do – what I have been trying to do these 30 years – is to see God face to face, to attain moksha. All that I do is directed to this same end.
- If you can rise above your karma, then you may not have to come back to this planet. You can go back to heaven, to be with God. I do not want to live as a human being forever on earth ...

Here is a famous prayer from a Hindu holy book:

> Lead me from lies to truth.
> Lead me from darkness to light.
> Lead me from death to life.

1 In small groups, design a spider-gram of all the most important things you want to do in your life. Which of these goals will last longest?

2 Write a sentence to explain what moksha is.

3 In groups, make a poster with the title 'Release'. Cut out pictures from newspapers to show some of the things people would like to be released from in life.

There are 3 ways for a Hindu to gain moksha:

1 The way of good deeds
2 The way of self-control and meditation
3 The way of love for God.

These ways are shown in the pictures below.

The first way is easy to understand. Hindus believe that if they are kind to others, they will become better people and have a better chance to escape rebirth.

In the second way, Hindus learn to control their bodies. This is called yoga. They do this so that they can concentrate on God. This is called meditation. In this way, they hope to become one with God.

The third way is chosen by many Hindus. They want to show their love for God in joyful worship. They believe that God loves them in return, and will take them to him when they die.

Good Works

Self-control and Meditation

You may need a teacher…

…To learn to control your body…

Meditation: Thinking only of God

Concentrate on this

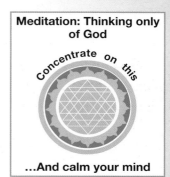

…And calm your mind

Love and Devotion

Parents love their children

…And children love their parents

God loves us… So we show our love for God

▲ *Ways to moksha*

25

1 Design THREE badges to stand for the 3 ways that lead to moksha.

2 Draw a picture strip with THREE more ideas of good works.

3 If you wanted to sit and think quietly, what object would you choose to look at? Draw it and explain why you chose it.

4 Which of the 3 ways would you choose? Give your reasons.

Hindus seem to worship many different gods. They have statues of gods and goddesses in their shrines. They have many stories about them in their holy books. **Yet Hinduism teaches that there is only one God!**

This story is about a child asking her grandmother questions about the gods:

> 'How many gods are there?'
> '3000 gods.'
> The child asked again, 'How many gods are there?'
> '300'
> Again, the child said, 'How many gods are there?'
> '3'
> One last time, the child asked the grandmother, 'How many gods are there?'
> 'One only!'

There are different ideas about how one God can be so many. Some believe that all the gods and goddesses are aspects of the one God, Brahman. Each shows a different side of God. One shows him as the creator, another as a loving friend and so on, just as a mother can also be a wife, a doctor and a friend. They are different aspects of the same person.

All these gods and goddesses help Hindus to come to know the one God, Brahman. Try to think of something that is in everything and is everywhere, but you can't see it, not even in your mind. That is what it is like to try to imagine Brahman. Did you find it impossible? Most people do.

Now think of the sun or the moon. Or look at the pictures in this chapter. That is much easier. So that is how many Hindus think of Brahman. They believe he is in everything, so anything can remind them of him.

Brahman may take the form of gods and goddesses. In the form of Brahma, God made the world. (So Brahma is one form of Brahman. Try not to confuse their names!) As Vishnu, God keeps the world going. (So Vishnu is one form of Brahman.) And as Shiva, God will destroy the world. (So Shiva is one form of Brahman.)

Hindus usually have a favourite form of Brahman. They keep a picture or statue of this god or goddess in their home. **Many Hindus choose either Shiva or Vishnu.**

> My favourite god is Shiva, because when we went to India my Mum bought me a necklace and Shiva was on it. I like him because at night, when I have bad thoughts, I think about him and they go away.

▲ *This priest worships Vishnu. We can tell by the shape of the white mark on his forehead*

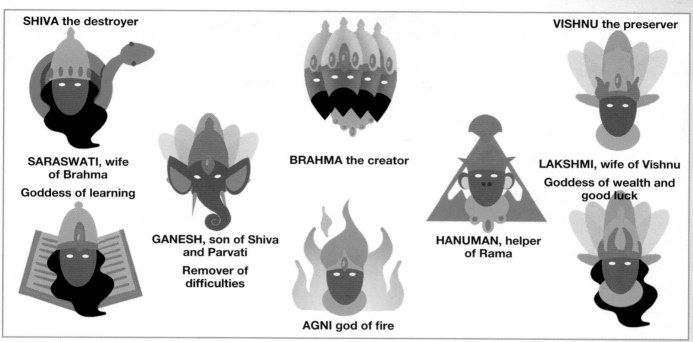

SHIVA the destroyer

SARASWATI, wife of Brahma

Goddess of learning

GANESH, son of Shiva and Parvati

Remover of difficulties

BRAHMA the creator

AGNI god of fire

HANUMAN, helper of Rama

VISHNU the preserver

LAKSHMI, wife of Vishnu

Goddess of wealth and good luck

▲ *Some of the Hindu gods and goddesses*

There are also symbols for Brahman. The most important of these is Aum. (Find where you have drawn this symbol in your book, from Chapter 2.)

> Aum means everything, God and the universe. It means all the good things. When you say Aum you don't think of any bad things.

1 Think of a word or phrase that could make you feel calm if you said it again and again (like the Hindu use of Aum). Write it on a page and make it look special.

2 How does Hinduism make it easier for people to think about God?

3 Draw your own picture of one of the Hindu ideas of God. Choose from this list:
- the Creator
- god of learning
- remover of difficulties.

◄ *Vishnu*

The picture above is of the god Vishnu. Hindus believe that Vishnu comes to earth to help in times of trouble. They believe that he has already appeared 9 times, and they speak of one still to come. These appearances take the form of animals and people.

Vishnu is speaking in this passage from the Hindu holy book, the *Gita*:

> If people stop worshipping God ... at that time, I Myself come down. I Myself appear millennium after millennium, to help good people, to destroy evil, and to save religion.
>
> Gita *4:7–8*

Look at the picture above. There are certain things that you often see on Hindu images. Here are some of them:
- many arms show that God has a lot to do;
- weapons in their hands show God's power over evil;
- crowns on their heads show God's importance;
- flowers round their necks show that God is worshipped;
- rich clothes and jewellery show the glory of God.

In this picture, Vishnu is seated on a big snake (a cobra). This shows his power.

The 10 appearances of Vishnu

1) **As a fish,** Vishnu saved Manu (the Indian version of Noah) from the great flood.

2) **As a tortoise,** Vishnu stirred up the sea to produce many wonderful things, such as the moon.

3) **As a boar,** Vishnu pulled the earth from under the sea with his tusks.

4) **As a man-lion,** Vishnu killed a demon who ruled the world. This demon had stopped people worshipping God.

5) **As a dwarf,** Vishnu asked a demon ruler to let him have as much land as he could cover in 3 steps. The demon laughed at his small size and agreed. Vishnu then grew to his full size and covered the whole world.

6) **As Parasu-rama,** Vishnu saved the priests from being killed by the soldier caste.

7) **As Rama,** Vishnu killed a demon king and saved his wife, Sita, from the demon.

8) **As Krishna,** Vishnu fought against evil and gave his teachings (in the *Gita*).

9) **As the Buddha,** Vishnu taught the way of inner peace.

10) **As Kalki,** Vishnu will return at the end of this age. He will bring an age of peace and holiness.

Some Hindus believe in one Supreme God. They believe that all the others are lesser beings (something like the saints and angels of Christianity).

Some believe that Vishnu is the Supreme God. They only have statues of Vishnu and the forms in which he has appeared. The main appearances are Krishna and Rama. Krishna is said to have lived about 5000 years ago. He was a cowherd. He is often shown playing a flute. Some Hindus see this as a symbol of heavenly music which he wants to give to the world.

---

1 Draw a comic strip of one of the 10 appearances of Vishnu

2 Imagine that you are Kalki, arriving on earth. What would you do to make the world a better place?

3 Krishna played the flute. Listen to some flute music. How would you describe it?

29

◀ *Rama's battle to rescue Sita*

Many Hindus want to love and worship God. They want to know God as a person and a friend. About 500 years ago, a man named Caitanya began worshipping Krishna in this way. He taught that the way to become close to God was to spend many hours each day chanting these names for God:

Hare Krishna, Hare Krishna,
Krishna, Krishna,
Hare, Hare,
Hare Rama, Hare Rama,
Rama, Rama,
Hare, Hare.

This movement still exists today. In 1965 it was brought to the West and now has centres throughout the world. A pop star, one of the Beatles, called George Harrison, became a Hare Krishna follower. He bought them a large house and estate just north of London. This is now one of the main centres of Hinduism in Britain. They also have a temple in the centre of London. Its followers can be seen on the streets of London, dressed in yellow robes, dancing and singing God's holy names.

◀ *Caitanya*

Some Hindus worship Shiva as the Supreme Lord, rather than Vishnu or Krishna. A verse from one of the Hindu holy books shows this:

> Love the Lord and be free.
> He is the One who appears as many ...
> May Lord Shiva, creator, destroyer,
> the beautiful and wise one,
> free us from the circle of birth and death.

The dancing figure of Shiva shows his great power over the world:

- He holds a drum in his right hand. This shows that he is the creator of the world. It is the beat of life – like a heart-beat.
- He dances, with his hair flying, as he holds all of nature in balance.
- He treads down the demon which could destroy the world he has created.
- Behind him is a circle of flames, to remind us about the circle of birth and death.

▲ *Lord Shiva*

Key words

Krishna
Shiva
Rama

1 Draw the picture of Shiva from this page. Label each of the details, saying what they mean.

2 Hindus have TWO ideas about how one God can be many.

i) Some believe that all the gods and goddesses are aspects of the one God.
ii) Some believe there is just one Supreme God, and all the rest are lesser beings. Which of these ideas do you think makes most sense?

Hindu ideas about God can be hard to understand. So they tell lots of stories, to make it easier.

The 5 Blind Men and an Elephant

5 holy men lived on the banks of the River Indus. They were all blind. One day, a tame elephant came down to the river. The men heard the noise and felt around them.

The first man felt its body, and said it was a wall of mud.

The second felt its tusks, and said they were 2 spears.

The third felt its trunk, and said it was a snake.

The fourth felt its tail, and said it was a piece of rope.

The last man held its leg, and said it was a tree.

Then a little child walked by and said, 'Why are you all holding the elephant?'

This story is about what God is like. It teaches people that when they try to understand God, they can only understand a part of him. It teaches them to be humble like the little child. They are not to think they have all the answers. They will never understand all there is to know about God and the universe.

The Butter Thief

When Krishna was a little boy he pulled over a large pot of butter and ate some. Then he ran off and fed some to the monkeys. His mother was angry and ran after him with a stick. When he started to cry, his mother felt sorry for him and did not hit him.

But she wanted to teach him a lesson. So she took a rope to tie him up. But when she tried to use it, it would not go round his body and meet up. She got a longer rope, but still it would not reach. At last, Krishna let himself be tied up. He realised that his mother was doing it for his own good, to teach him right from wrong.

The meaning of this story is like the last one. People want to understand God fully. It is as if they want to tie him down. They cannot do it. They can only understand what God allows them to.

▶ *Krishna runs away from his mother*

The Universe in Krishna's Mouth

The child Krishna played with the other boys and girls in his village. He also played in the mud with his brother. One day the village children told his mother that he had eaten some dirt. Krishna said he hadn't. 'Open your mouth, then, and let me see!' said his mother. But when Krishna opened his mouth, she saw the whole universe inside! Then she knew that this was God in human form. She bowed down and worshipped him. But Krishna made her forget what had happened and she continued to behave as his mother.

This story teaches that God can be found in the small, ordinary things of life.

Krishna the Cowherd Boy

Krishna was a cowherd as a boy. He played games with the other boys as they took the cows to the river. When they got tired, Krishna took out his bamboo flute and started to play.

The music was so beautiful that the river ran backwards. Birds fell from the sky in a trance and the cows stood still. When the music stopped, all went back to normal. But now no one was tired.

The meaning of this story is that God is beautiful and full of life. He draws people to him and they fall in love with him. When people are in the presence of God, all other pleasures are forgotten.

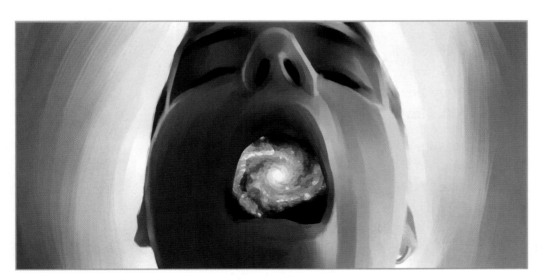

▲ *The universe in Krishna's mouth*

1 Act out the story of the blind men and the elephant. Have a narrator to say what the meaning is.

2 a) Think of the most beautiful place you have ever been to. How did it make you feel?
b) Ask someone who worships God to describe how it makes them feel.

The Rasa Dance

One moonlit night, Krishna played beautiful music on his flute. The cowherd girls heard the music. They stopped what they were doing and ran towards it, in the forest. They found Krishna by the riverside. They danced and talked and joked with him.

One by one, each girl began to feel proud that Krishna was with her. But then Krishna disappeared. They looked everywhere for him. Then they found 2 sets of footprints. One belonged to Krishna and one to his favourite girl, Radha. They felt jealous of Radha, until they found her on her own. She was crying because Krishna had left her too and they felt sorry for her.

They were sorry that they had been proud and jealous. They sang Krishna's name. Then he appeared among them, smiling. He started a dance and soon there were lots of him and he was dancing with each of the girls! This was the Rasa dance.

This story teaches people that God goes away when they become proud. Sometimes religion makes people proud. They have to learn that they do not deserve God's love. It is given freely.

The Cowherd Girls

One day the cowherd girls were bathing in the river. Krishna decided to play a trick on them. He took their clothes.

Krishna said he would return their clothes, but they had to come out of the water one by one. He called each girl out of the water by name and asked her to stand before him. They came out, one by one, covering themselves with their hands. But Krishna asked them to worship him, so they had to put their hands together, raise them above their heads, and bow before him.

As they worshipped him, he threw down their clothes, and they became his brides. Their shame was turned to joy, for this was what they wanted more than anything in the world.

The meaning of this story is that we cannot hide anything from God. The girls are like our souls. The story teaches that God sees what we are like inside, just as if we were standing naked before him. The end of the story shows that he loves each one of us.

1 Talk about what it means to say that someone saw right through you. Think about a time when this happened to you. How did it make you feel?

2 Choose to work on either pride or jealousy. In groups of 2 or 3, invent a drama to show how it can make people unhappy.

◄ *Krishna appeared with each cowherd girl and danced with her*

◀ *Life is like a journey . . .*

Life is like a journey. We set out on life; grow and change; learn new skills; become adults and may marry and have children. We grow old. And one day we die, at our journey's end. People often have ceremonies for each new step in life. The most common are for:

- the birth of a baby
- getting married
- becoming an adult
- death.

In Hinduism there are 16 important steps in life.

TASK

Talk about ceremonies to mark either birth, marriage or death.

- Where do they take place?
- What do people wear?
- Do they use any special things in the ceremony?
- Do they say special words?

---

1 a) Draw a path of some kind (eg a road, railway, space journey). Mark on it special things that have happened to you in life so far. (These could be birthdays, holidays, presents, trips or people you have met. They could be sad things like the death of a pet or an illness.)
b) Which of these steps in your life do you think are most important?

2 In groups, make up a ceremony for 'coming of age', when young people begin to be treated as adults. (You need to think about the 4 questions in the Task above.)

● Birth and Childhood

Look at the Hindu steps on this page. The first 3 take place even before the child is born. When a Hindu baby is born, the parents tell the priest. He draws up a horoscope for the baby. He does this because many Hindus believe that the stars and planets affect our lives. The priest uses the horoscope to tell the parents the first letter of the baby's name.

Hindu babies are often named after gods such as Krishna, or goddesses such as Lakshmi. Some other names are Rani for a girl (meaning 'princess') and Deepak for a boy (meaning 'light').

> **Key words**
>
> **ceremony**
> **horoscope**
> **holy**
> **sacred**

▲ *The first haircut*

36

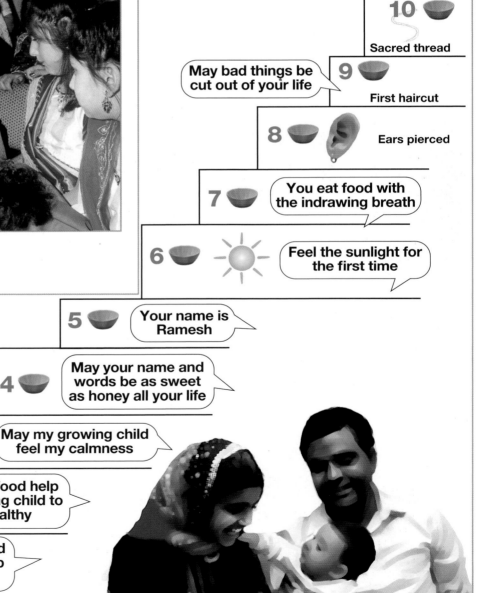

10 Sacred thread

May bad things be cut out of your life

9 First haircut

8 Ears pierced

7 You eat food with the indrawing breath

6 Feel the sunlight for the first time

5 Your name is Ramesh

4 May your name and words be as sweet as honey all your life

3 May my growing child feel my calmness

2 May this food help my growing child to be healthy

1 May we have a child to love and bring up to live a good life

▲ *The steps of childhood*

● The Sacred Thread

There is a special day for many Hindu boys between their 8th and 11th birthdays. It is another important step in life for them. It is the day when they first start to wear the sacred thread.

This thread is made from 3 strands of cotton. It reminds the boy that he has 3 duties:

1 to God, for giving him everything he needs
2 to his parents, for giving birth to him
3 to his teacher for teaching him about religion.

It also reminds him to control 3 things:

1 what he thinks
2 what he says
3 what he does.

The sacred thread ceremony takes place at home. Usually the priest puts it on. It goes over the boy's left shoulder and under his right arm. He wears it all his life, but changes it every year.

The sacred thread ceremony marks the boy's coming of age. He is now old enough to obey the rules of his religion.

This Hindu mother in England explains why her 2 sons do not wear the sacred thread.

> Our boys have not taken the thread because they eat meat. If they take the thread they have to give up meat. I don't want to force them. It's something they must choose.

◀ *The sacred thread ceremony*

---

1 Look at the words in the word box.
   a) Which TWO words mean the same?
   b) Write a sentence for each of the first TWO words to explain their meanings.

2 Find out how your name was chosen. If you could choose a new name, what would it be, and why?

3 Horoscopes claim to be able to tell the future. Talk with your partner about whether you want to know your future.

4 Hindu boys thank God, their parents and their teachers for all that they have in life. If you could choose THREE people to thank, who would they be?

● Marriage

One of the biggest steps in life is choosing who to marry. If you make the right choice, you will want to stay with that person until one of you dies. But an unwise choice can cause much unhappiness.

Most Hindus think it is their duty to marry. But they also think it is easy for young people to choose the wrong person. So Hindu marriages are usually arranged by the parents.

They will choose someone with a similar background and education. If they have these things in common, they are likely to get on. Love will come later.

Modern Hindu parents usually let the couple meet. Then they give them the right to decide if they want to marry each other.

A Hindu boy tells us what happened in his family.

> When my sister got married, that was arranged. My whole family went to his house first. We met his parents and his family. Then we went home and we phoned them afterwards to tell them what we thought. They said, 'Yes' and we said, 'Yes'.
>
> So my sister got married. The groom sat on the stage. He wore a garland of flowers. People threw money on the stage and they collected it all for the bride and groom.

This Hindu woman remembers a family wedding in Southampton.

> The bridegroom came on a horse. They have to have something covering their face and they should sit on a horse. Not everybody in England does, but he was the only son, so they had the proper ceremony.
>
> There was a party with music and dancing. Nobody had drink. We're not supposed to have drink. But nowadays, children born here are a bit different. They say, 'When we go to our friends' marriages and parties, they have drinks.' So sometimes you have to go along with that.

Key words

sari
henna
arranged marriage

▶ *This Hindu bride is ready for her wedding. She wears a beautiful red sari and many jewels. The red patterns on her hands are made with a dye called henna. They are signs that she is starting a new life. Red is a lucky colour, the colour of life.*

Hindu weddings often take place at night, when the pole star comes out. The promises they make to each other should be like the pole star, and never change.

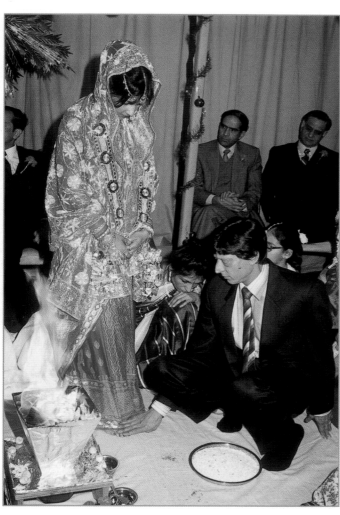

▲ *A newly married Hindu couple*

At a Hindu wedding, the bride and groom take 7 steps around the sacred fire. You can see the fire in the photo. It reminds Hindus that God is there with them.

The 7 steps are for the hopes that they have for their married life:

1 food
2 energy
3 wealth
4 happiness
5 children
6 seasons (long life)
7 friendship.

As they take these steps, they are tied together by a scarf. This shows that they are joining their lives in marriage. After the last step they are husband and wife.

Notice the plate of rice in the photo. This is thrown over them to wish them many children. How has the West adopted this practice?

1 Talk with your partner about the meaning of the first TWO words in the word box. They are both to do with the Indian way of life.

2 Match the things in List A with their meanings in List B:

List A
- patterns on hands
- 4th step
- pole star
- final step

List B
- promises will never change
- friendship
- happiness
- starting new life.

3 Write out the 7 steps on 7 small pieces of paper. Talk about them with your partner. Then arrange them in order, with the most important first.

● Old Age and Death

Most Hindus spend their lives with their families. But some withdraw from family life when their children have grown up and married. They have more time then to spend on religion.

Sometimes, they leave home altogether. A man may go on his own, or his wife might go with him. They go and live in the forest or travel to holy places. They spend their time in prayer and reading holy books.

A few Hindus finally give up everything. They are called sadhus, or holy men. They often have only a cloth round their waist, a food bowl and a water pot. They don't want anything to come between them and God.

Sadhus are usually old men, in the last stage of their lives. But sometimes a young man becomes a sadhu. This one explains why he has given up everything in life:

By worshipping daily and living a sadhu's life, you meet God himself. God takes a sadhu and that man is free ... He will not have to be reborn into human form again.

There are many sadhus. For 24 hours of the day they think only of God ... Some go a little way, some go half-way, and some cross over completely to God ... I hope that I will cross over. But it is in God's hands.

40

◀ A Hindu sadhu in Nepal

Death is the last of the 16 steps in life. When a Hindu dies, the body is washed and dressed in new clothes. The family brings flowers to put round it. The body is burned on a funeral pyre which is lit by the eldest son. (You can see this in the photo.) The ashes are scattered in a river, because rivers are holy to Hindus.

At the end of the ceremony, the priest chants this prayer:

> The soul is never born, and never dies.
> Once living, it never stops living.
> As a man lays aside his worn-out clothes
> And puts on others that are new
> So the soul within the body lays aside that body
> And puts on another body that is new.

This teenager remembers how he felt after his grandfather's death:

> I remembered how fond he had been of us, his grandchildren, and I felt very upset. But we must not be too sad about his death. His life had been a good one, and we feel sure that his soul will get a good rebirth.

Some bodies are not cremated, because they are thought to be without sin. These are the bodies of babies, young children and very holy people. Holy men are sometimes buried. The bodies of babies and small children are tied to a heavy stone and sunk in a river. A lamp is floated downstream on sticks. It is a symbol of the baby's soul.

▲ *The funeral pyre is lit by the eldest son*

Key words

sadhu
funeral pyre
cremation

1 Explain what a sadhu is. Do you think their life is hard or easy?

2 The funeral prayer in the box speaks of worn-out clothes and new clothes.
   a) What are the worn-out clothes of the soul?
   b) What will the soul's new clothes be?

3 What do you think happens to a person's soul at death?

A pilgrimage is a religious journey. **Many Hindus travel to religious places. It is an important part of their religion.** They like to go on pilgrimage, but it is not the same as a holiday. They like to see new places, but they do not lie on the beach, or dance in clubs. The main reason for going is to get closer to God.

Most pilgrimages end at a temple. There are temples everywhere in India, but 4 are extra special. They are at:

1 Puri
2 Rameshwaram
3 Dwarka
4 Badrinath.

TASK

Look back at the map in Chapter 1, and find these 4 places. They are in 4 different parts of India, thousands of miles apart.

Every Hindu would like to visit these 4 holy cities. Many save up all their lives to do it. There are many hardships on the journey. But Hindus put up with them because they are doing the journey for God.

It is not only the poor who have hardships, as this pilgrim explains:

A rich person might go barefoot, even in very cold weather. The idea is that we have to forget about our comfort. Through our own suffering, we are able to understand other people's suffering as well.

▶ *The temple at Badrinath is visited by many pilgrims*

Many rivers are places of pilgrimage. The Ganges is the holiest river of all. Hindus call it Mother Ganga. All Hindus would like to bathe in this river. They believe it will wash away their sins. This was written in praise of the River Ganges:

> Mother Ganga, I bow down to you. Just the touch of your holy waters makes humans, and even animals, become as pure and as beautiful as Shiva.

Two Hindu children tell us about their visit to the Ganges:

- Pooja: It comes from the Himalayas. The snow melts and comes down.

- Anuj: It's a river from Heaven. Shiva brought it down to wash all the sins away.

Another Hindu describes his pilgrimage to Varanasi. This is the holiest city on the River Ganges:

> I thought there might be just a few people there. But there were thousands of people. And so early in the morning!
>
> When I went there I had my first bath in the Ganges. I was thrilled that I was able to bathe in this sacred river. It was a great feeling. It was like going to Heaven.

Key words

pilgrimage
pilgrim

◀ *Hindus in the River Ganges*

1 Match the words in List A with their meanings in List B.

List A	List B
• Varanasi	• an important temple
• pilgrimage	• where the Ganges begins
• Mother Ganga	• a holy city
• Himalayas	• a religious journey
• Puri	• the holiest river

2 Using the map on page 4, draw a map of India, and put on it:
- the TWO main rivers: the Indus and the Ganges
- the FOUR main holy cities (listed on page 42).

3 Explain why Hindus go on pilgrimage.

In Puri there is a temple to Jagannath. This is a giant image of Krishna. ('Jagannath' gives us the word 'juggernaut'.) Every year the huge statue is carried through the streets on a lorry. It is just like a big carnival.

There is an old Hindu story about Jagannath. It teaches us about Hindu worship:

> One day a rich man came to the temple in Puri. He wanted to give a huge sum of money to pay for a gift of food for the god. But he wanted to use it up in one go.
>
> At first the priests were very happy. But when they thought about it, they knew they could not use up all that money. They prayed to Jagannath for wisdom, and asked the rich man to wait until they had an answer.
>
> 3 days later, the head priest had a dream. This was his answer to the rich man: 'Lord Jagannath says that you should pay for just one nut as your offering.'
>
> The rich man was insulted. He could give much more than that! But the priest hadn't finished. He said that the nut must be covered with a finely ground pearl – so rare that it is only found under the skin on an elephant's head.
>
> The rich man was angry. He would have to buy many elephants, and he still might not find the pearl. He had so much money, yet he could not give a single nut to Lord Jagannath!
>
> Then he saw the truth. He ran to the temple and threw himself on the ground before Jagannath. He was sorry that he had tried to show off with his money. He should have known that God only accepts gifts which are given in love. He said, 'Everything belongs to you, so what can I give except my heart?' And from that day on, he used his money to feed the poor.

In the Hindu holy book, the *Gita*, Krishna says: 'A person may give me even a leaf, a flower, a fruit, or a drop of water. When it is offered with love, I will accept it.'

▲ *Hindus in Britain at the Jagannath festival*

1 Write a sentence about each of the words in the word box. Show that you understand the words.

2 Use coloured magazines to cut out pictures of leaves, flowers and fruits. Make a picture with these and draw in a small bowl of water. Then copy out Krishna's saying beneath it.

44

◀ *At festivals, Hindus decorate their homes with special patterns. They are called Rangoli patterns. They make them on the ground outside their houses. They are to welcome their friends to their home. The patterns are made with coloured powder, rice or sand.*

TASK

Make a class list of all the festivals you celebrate in a year, beginning with New Year. Tick any that are religious festivals. Copy the list into your books.

Hinduism has more festivals than any other religion. A festival happens every day in some part of India! But not all Hindus take part in every festival.

People celebrate in different ways in different places. The same festival can last between one and 5 days, depending where it is held.

There are 2 main reasons for Hindu festivals:

1 to celebrate the lives of the gods and goddesses, and the lives of holy people;
2 to celebrate the seasons, like the coming of Spring.

● **New Year**

The Hindu New Year is at the beginning of the Indian summer, in March or April. (But in some parts of India it is celebrated at other times!) Some Hindu families make a special banner to welcome the New Year. They make it by tying different things to a bamboo pole. They are:

● a piece of new cloth
● a cooking pot
● some pieces of sugar
● a leafy branch.

Each of these things stands for something they hope that God will give them in the coming year.

45

---

1 Put the title 'Hindu New Year'.
Copy out the list of things on the New Year banner. Talk with your teacher about what they could mean. Then write down the meaning beside each thing.

2 Think of FOUR things you would wish for at New Year. Draw a banner with 4 things on it to stand for your 4 wishes.

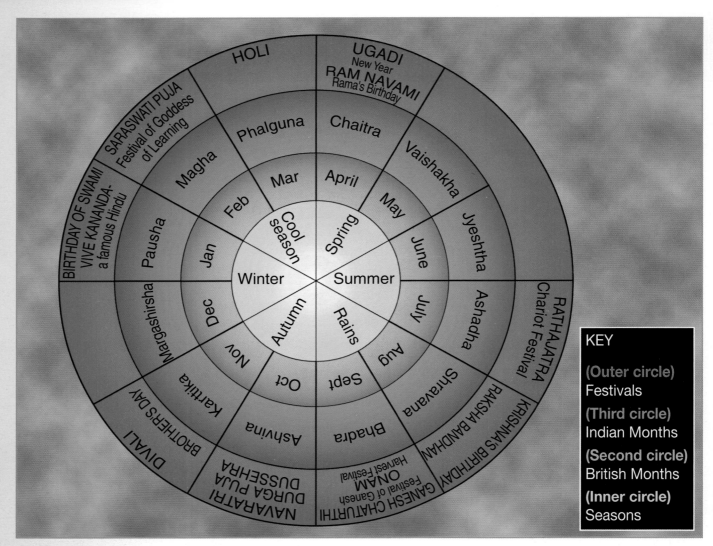

▲ *Calendar of the main Hindu festivals*

The calendar wheel shows (from outer to inner):

Outer circle — Festivals: HOLI, UGADI New Year, RAM NAVAMI Rama's Birthday, SARASWATI PUJA Festival of Goddess of Learning, BIRTHDAY OF SWAMI VIVE KANANDA- a famous Hindu, RATHAJATRA Chariot Festival, RAKSHA BANDHAN, KRISHNA'S BIRTHDAY, GANESH CHATURTHI Festival of Ganesh, ONAM Harvest Festival, NAVARATRI DURGA PUJA DUSSEHRA, DIVALI, BROTHER'S DAY

Third circle — Indian Months: Phalguna, Chaitra, Vaishakha, Jyeshtha, Ashadha, Shravana, Bhadra, Ashvina, Karttika, Margashirsha, Pausha, Magha

Second circle — British Months: Mar, April, May, June, July, Aug, Sept, Oct, Nov, Dec, Jan, Feb

Inner circle — Seasons: Cool season, Spring, Summer, Rains, Autumn, Winter

KEY

(Outer circle)
Festivals

(Third circle)
Indian Months

(Second circle)
British Months

(Inner circle)
Seasons

46

● Brothers and Sisters

There are 2 festivals for brothers and sisters.

Brothers' Day

Brothers and sisters give each other presents, and the family has a special meal. The girl prays that her brothers will live for a long time. She rubs yellow powder onto their foreheads and sings this prayer:

> I pray God to save you from disease and accidental death. May your life have a golden future.

Raksha Bandhan

The boy's sister ties a bracelet around his wrist. In turn, he promises to protect her. It reminds Hindus of the story that Vishnu gave the god Indra's wife a thread to tie on Indra's wrist. It brought him good luck.

> I take a bracelet made of string. It's got a flower on it. I put it on my brother's wrist and he keeps it on for about a week. I give my brother some sweets. He gives me some money and promises to look after me.

1 Talk about ways in which a brother can protect his sister.

2 Work out a role-play in which a sister looks after her brother, or the other way round.

Rama and Ravana

The story so far...

Rama's wife, Sita, has been kidnapped by the evil king Ravana.

Rama and his brother search for Sita...

They ask the king of the birds...

I tried to save Sita – Ravana has taken her south

I will send Hanuman – he will find Sita in 30 days

...And the king of the monkeys

After 28 days...

I have failed – I deserve to die!

Ravana and Sita are on the island of Lanka

Hanuman finds Sita and returns to Rama

Ravana, the demon king, fights Rama

At last... Good has beaten evil

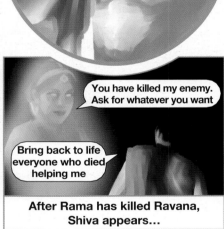

You have killed my enemy. Ask for whatever you want

Bring back to life everyone who died helping me

After Rama has killed Ravana, Shiva appears...

Rama and Sita return home

▲ *How Rama defeated Ravana*

The story of Rama and Sita is the best-known story in Hinduism. In some parts of India it is told at a festival called Dasshera. A Hindu tells us about it:

> Even today, this story is acted out in every city and village in India. It celebrates the victory of Good over Evil.
>
> When I was a child, we made rough clay statues of the demon, Ravana. We put them on the ground. Then, shouting, 'Kill, kill, kill', we would hop on our bikes and ride all over them.

Often, a huge paper statue of Ravana is burned. It is filled with fireworks, so there is plenty of noise.

● Divali

Some Hindus remember the story of Rama and Sita at the festival of Divali. This is a festival of lights. It takes place in late autumn. The word Divali means a row of lights. Hindus decorate their homes with rows of lights. In India, they use little oil lamps, called divas. In the West, they may use electric lights, as in the photo below.

A Hindu remembers Divali when she was a child:

> Nothing was lit until after the evening prayers – and after my mother had told us the Divali story. We would run outside and begin lighting the lamps. Soon the whole house would be glittering. Then it was time for the fireworks. My father would aim a fiery rocket towards the sky. I would take a long sparkler, stand in the middle of the lawn and then turn round and round and round until I seemed encircled by my own glow.

Light is the opposite of darkness. Good is the opposite of evil. So the Divali lights stand for the victory of good over evil.

▲ *A house lit up at Divali*

Holi

Holi is a spring festival. It is named after the evil Princess Holika. She tried to kill her nephew in a bonfire, to stop him worshipping Vishnu. But she died in the fire herself.

Holi begins on the night of a full moon. It lasts for up to 5 days. In the evening, the priest lights a huge bonfire. This is called burning Holi. Often men and boys dance round the fire.

The next morning, people play tricks on each other. It is called playing Holi. Hindus throw coloured powder and water at each other. It is done to remember how Krishna liked to joke with people. A Hindu tells us how she played Holi as a child:

> A special ugly colour was made for our enemies. We mixed grease with mud, slime and purple dye.
>
> For our best friends, we made a golden paint. We mixed real gold powder and oil in a small jar.

By the afternoon it is time for a bath and clean clothes. Luckily, the colour usually washes out easily. Then they have a special festival meal.

▲ *Young people throw dye over each other at Holi*

Most Hindu festivals are linked to stories. It is a way of teaching people about religion. Many Hindu stories are about the victory of good over evil. They give people hope for a better future.

The festivals also turn people's minds to God. They are special times to worship him.

1 Look at the story of Rama and Sita on page 47. Act it out in class.
2 Ravana was a 10-headed demon! Design your own idea of an evil power. You can use old symbols like the skull and crossbones. Or you can use modern ideas.
3 Do you know any stories about good winning over evil? List their titles.

▲ *A Hindu family shrine inside the home*

TASK

Are there any places in your home that are used for special occasions?

Hindus have special places where they can pray and think about God. It does not have to be a temple. **The home is the centre of a Hindu's religion. So every Hindu home has a shrine.** A shrine is a special place for worship. In a big house, it might be a room. In a small house, it might be just a shelf.

We've got a little shrine that my Dad made. We put a candle in it and my Mum sings a holy song. We all sit down and start praying.

Hindu shrines have statues and pictures of the gods. The mother usually looks after the family shrine. This is what she does during worship:

- lights a candle in the morning;
- washes and dresses the image of God;
- offers flowers and burns incense;
- offers food.

I take some food and put it on a plate in front of our god. I sprinkle some holy water. I leave part of the food there for the god. I take the rest back and mix it in with the food for the family.

God gives us food, so we just imagine that we're giving God a welcome by offering food. It's a way of saying 'Thank you for everything you've done.'

Hindus wash themselves before they worship. They take a bath or shower every morning and put on clean clothes. In India, many go down to the river to bathe.

Hindus try to pray 3 times a day. Then they feel that their minds are clean.

There are 2 main kinds of prayer in Hinduism:

1 to praise God for life
2 to ask God for something.

People may ask God for help in trouble, or that someone who is ill might get better. Or they may ask to become a better person. A Hindu girl and her mother explain:

Mother: I just tell them, when they get up: 'Pray to God, let us do good things and be kind to people. Give us a good day.'

Pooja: At night when I go to bed, I close my eyes and say Aum 3 times. Then I am quiet for 5 minutes and say Aum again. Then I feel tired and peaceful.

Hindus say a special prayer each morning. It ends like this:

> Peace be in the heavens; peace be on earth.
> May the waters flow peacefully.
> May the plants grow peacefully ...
> And may that peace come to us.
> Aum. Peace. Peace. Peace.

There are other kinds of worship that Hindus do:
- they sit quietly
- they read from the holy books
- they sing the names of God.

> We must not forget our God for a single minute ... We are busy doing everything, our dusting or our cooking. But if we want peace, we remember we are doing it for God.

▲ *Worship at home*

1 What are the TWO main reasons why Hindus pray?

2 Design a 'thank-you box'.
Decorate a box with colourful paper or your own artwork. Inside the box, place photos, objects, letters, etc. It can be anything to remind you of people and things you are thankful for.

3 Draw or paint a picture to illustrate some of the words about peace in the first box on this page.

Some young people were asked to design their ideal space for worship in their homes. Some imagined a quiet place in the garden, or in their loft or shed.

One girl said she would sit on bean bags, light floating candles, burn incense and listen to music with the lights dimmed.

Key words

incense
shrine

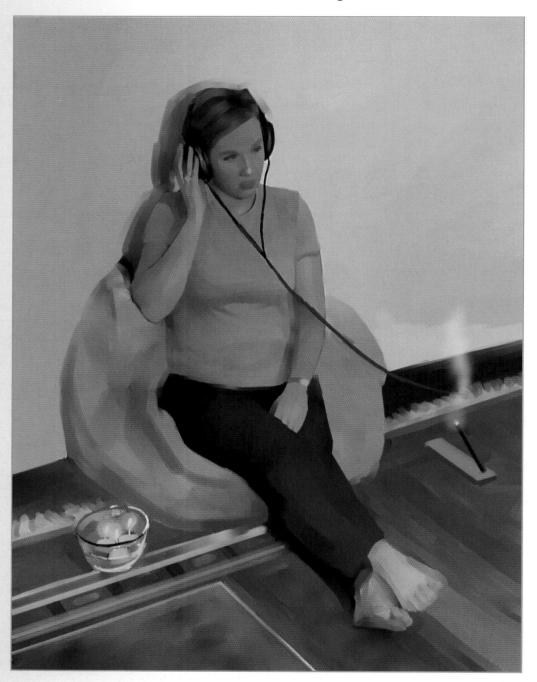

▲ *Chill out! Incense, music and candlelight*

1 Design your own special place in your home. Would it be like the one in the picture? What would make it special to you?

A Hindu temple is called a mandir. **Hindus think of a mandir as the home of God.** They believe that God is everywhere, but some places are extra special. Every temple has at least one shrine. This is where an image of God is used for worship. Temples vary in size. Some villages have a simple hut for the image. But most temples in India are very grand.

Worship in a temple is like worship at home, but it is led by a priest. The priest looks after each image of God, while the people come and go. He wakes it in the morning, and washes and dresses it. He draws a curtain across the shrine to give it a rest in the afternoon. He closes the curtain again at night.

Hindus can go to a temple at any time of day. They go on their own or with their family. They remove their shoes. They may also wash their hands. They ring a bell to say they have arrived. They bring an offering of food, flowers or money. They may walk round the shrine. There is lots to do and lots to see. Hindu temples are usually noisy places. People praise God with singing, clapping, musical instruments and gongs.

▶ *Joyful worship in a Hindu temple*

▲ *A priest performs the arti ceremony*

In the next 2 boxes, you can read what this means for them.

> God is in the form of light. The fire, you know, is a very holy fire. It can purify everything and that is why it is lit.

> You almost touch the flame with your hand, and then you just bring your hands to your head. It's as if God is actually in the flame and he's giving you the blessing.

Hindus usually give something to God in the temple, however small. It is the thought that counts. Hindus believe that God knows what is in their hearts.

> A person may offer me even a leaf, a flower, a fruit or a drop of water. When it is offered with love, I will accept it.

People come and go at Hindu temples. But there is always a crowd for the arti ceremony. The priest uses a special oil lamp with several flames. He stands facing each image of God in turn. He rings a bell with one hand. At the same time, he makes circles with the lamp in his other hand. When the fire has been offered to God, the lamp is taken to each person in turn. (You can see this in the photo.)

It may seem strange for Hindus to offer God a tiny flame, when they believe that he created the sun. Or for them to offer God light, when they believe that he gives light and life. It is like a little child who picks a flower and offers it to his mother. This will mean much more to her than the most beautiful bunches of flowers.

Key words

mandir
arti

---

1 Write a sentence for each word in the word box. Show that you understand what the words mean.

2 Hindus treat the images as if God is really present in them. List FOUR things they do for the images.

carvings and statues. The statues near the ground are of animals. Those higher up are of humans. And the statues at the top of the building are of the gods. This is based on the old idea that the gods live high up.

The inner shrine of the temple is the 'womb'. This is where the image of the god is kept. A tower goes up above this.

The hall in front of the shrine is covered and held up by pillars.

▲ *This Hindu temple is in India. The first temple like this in Europe was built recently in north London*

A Hindu temple is seen as a place where heaven meets earth. Many are shaped like mountains. They are covered with

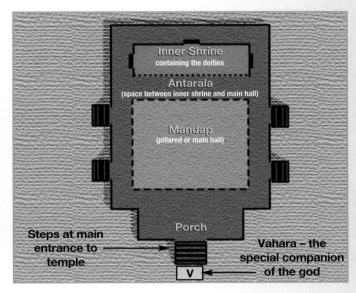

Inner Shrine
containing the deities

Antarala
(space between inner shrine and main hall)

Mandap
(pillared or main hall)

Porch

Steps at main entrance to temple

Vahara – the special companion of the god

V

▲ *The layout of some Hindu temples*

1 **a)** Copy the plan of a Hindu temple and label each part.

  b) Put numbers on the plan to show which part you think

    (i)   forms the boundary of the temple

    (ii) contains the image of the temple's special god

    (iii) is the place where shoes are left

    (iv) is the symbol of a mountain.

2 The temple is like a mountain reaching up to heaven.

  Talk about a time when you climbed to the top of a mountain or big hill.

  How did it feel? Did it give you a sense of greatness or power?

> God lives where women are treated with respect.
>
> *The Laws of Manu*

Hinduism teaches that men and women are equally important.

The mother is very important. She is in charge of the home. She is the one who keeps the religion going in the home. She brings up the children. And she is the one who often takes care of the money.

The father is also important. He usually goes out to work and supports the family.

But a Hindu woman always depends on a man. She is too important to be left on her own. Hinduism teaches that women should be looked after. In return, she should be loyal and loving to her husband:

> Father protects her in childhood, husband in youth, and sons in old age; a woman deserves to be looked after.

Up until the 19th century, it was usually only boys who went to school. Girls stayed at home. They learnt how to cook and do the housework. They also learnt about religion, art and music. Women had an important role in passing on the Hindu religion.

Today, Hindu girls also go to school. Many go on to college or university. They follow the same careers as men.

Modern Hindu women seek more equality with men. The Indian law now treats them equally. Women can vote in elections. India had a woman prime minister in the 20th century. Her name was Indira Gandhi.

Even in the past, there were some women who were different. They wrote books, or fought battles, as well as running their homes! But even those who were happy at home were not 'doormats'. The very old stories of Hinduism tell of a beautiful woman called Draupadi. Some soldiers raped her. When they all died in battle, it was seen as their punishment. And she knocked out a famous warrior with one punch!

▲ *Draupadi was no weak and shy woman*

Hindu widows used to have a very hard time, and some still do. It used to be taught that Hindu women should only marry once. If her husband died when she was still young, she had to dress plainly and live with her husband's family. She could not remarry.

In the past, it was the custom for some high-caste Hindus to throw themselves on their husband's funeral pyre and burn themselves to death. They did not want to go on living once their husband had died. This was known as sati, meaning 'devoted wife'. Some women were forced to die in this way. The British rulers of India stopped this custom in 1829.

This was made illegal in 1961, but it is still a common practice. Some poor families despair if they have too many daughters. It has led to terrible cases where baby girls are murdered or abandoned.

Another problem is that families can get greedy. They demand some more money after the wedding. If it is not given, they arrange an 'accident' for the wife. The son is then free to remarry and collect another dowry.

For over a century, Hindu women have led campaigns against injustices like this. Some things have changed to make their lives better. But more needs to be done.

> **Key words**
> sati
> dowry

▲ Handprints on a wall in memory of sati victims in the past

Another Hindu custom is to give a dowry (a payment) when a daughter gets married. The original idea was that parents would give their daughter gifts when she married. It was to show their love for her as she left for her new home with her husband's family. The parents would give whatever they could afford.

In later years, the system changed. The bride's parents were often asked to give a large dowry to the husband and his family.

▲ Indira Gandhi (no relation to Mahatma) became India's first woman Prime Minister in 1966

Hinduism has goddesses as well as gods. The goddesses can show the feminine side of God. So Shiva's gentle wife, Parvati, shows the kind and gentle side of God.

Some goddesses show that women can be strong and determined. Just look at the goddess Durga in this Hindu comic strip:

TALES OF DURGA

THEN TO THE AMAZEMENT OF SHUMBHA, THE VARIOUS SHAKTIS MERGED INTO DURGA.

SEIZING DURGA, SHUMBHA ROSE INTO THE SKY.

AFTER A FIERCE BATTLE IN MID-AIR, DURGA FLUNG THE ASURA DOWN ...

...AND SLEW HIM WITH HER SPEAR. REJOICING, THE DEVAS HEADED BY INDRA APPEARED ON THE SCENE.

WE SALUTE YOU, O MOTHER DURGA, DESTROYER OF EVIL.

31

▲ *Durga defeats the enemy of the gods*

The story in the comic strip is about Mahisha, the buffalo demon. He conquered the world, and wanted to conquer heaven. The 3 main gods, Brahma, Shiva and Vishnu, poured their power into a beautiful woman, called Durga. Durga was a goddess who refused to marry. She was strong and assertive. She was given Shiva's armour and a weapon from each god. As the comic strip shows, she fought Mahisha and killed him.

Some Hindu women look up to Durga and want to be like her.

▼ *Krishna and Radha*

Some Hindus consider Krishna to be the supreme God. He is often shown with his partner Radha. He loves her, and she worships him. But in one way, she is the more powerful. For Krishna is under the influence of love.

Krishna's love for Radha stands for God's love for the universe. The universe praises God in return.

1 Do you think women are treated equally in our society today? Can you think of any jobs where women still find it difficult to be accepted?

2 Goddesses show the feminine side of God.
a) When you think of God as a woman, what qualities come to mind?
b) Draw an image of God as Mother.

When Gandhi was shot dead in 1948, Nehru the Prime Minister said: 'The light has gone out of our lives.'

The huge crowd in the photo gathered for his funeral. They came from all over the world. But most were Hindus. They came to say goodbye to the man who had led India to independence. They called him Bapu, or Father. Many believed he was a saint.

Gandhi was born in 1869. He was just 13 when he married – his wife was the same age.

In 1888 Gandhi studied law in England. Later he became a lawyer in South Africa. He spoke out for the rights of Indians living there. Even at this early stage, Gandhi was prepared to break the law, but never to use violence.

Gandhi went home to India in 1915. He set up a religious community. It was based on his beliefs. Everyone there was equal. Life was simple. The morning prayer meeting always had these words:

We will be non-violent; we will be truthful; we will not steal; we will not keep more than we need ... we will work with our hands; we will eat simple foods ... we will work to set the Untouchables free.

Gandhi did not agree with the caste system. He wanted the Untouchables to be able to go into the temples. He wanted them to mix freely with other Hindus.

▲ *Gandhi's funeral*

He took a family of Untouchables into his community. He gave them a new name. He called them Harijans. This means Children of God.

In 1932 Gandhi went on a fast to protest about the treatment of the Untouchables. He was willing to die for them. This is what he said:

I believe that if untouchability is rooted out, it will cleanse Hinduism of a terrible crime ... My cry will rise to the throne of the Almighty God.

Key words

independence
fast

59

Gandhi's fast did bring about some changes. Untouchables were allowed into temples. They could walk on any road. They could draw water from any well. But not everyone agreed. Life is still difficult for many of them. A Harijan woman who lived in Gandhi's community as a girl, spoke many years later of her problems:

> I can't persuade my son to marry. He's confused about his caste. You see, my children's father was a Brahmin. Bapu arranged my marriage to him. But people here still hold it against my children that their mother was born a Harijan.

An example of Gandhi's non-violent action was the Salt March of 1930. It was a protest against a tax that the British rulers had put on salt. In a hot country like India, everyone uses a lot of salt.

Gandhi led a long march to the sea. When they got there, they made salt by boiling the sea water. Later, they marched on the salt factory. They tried to organise a 'sit in'. But as they entered one by one, they were arrested or beaten. Not once did the protesters use violence. Ordinary people were impressed. The rulers were shown to be bullies. It led to a change in the Salt Law.

▲ *The Salt March, 1930*

Gandhi is remembered for his non-violent action. He wasn't afraid to stand up against wrong, but he always refused to use violence. He believed in 'the force of truth'. He believed that truth and right were on his side. These sayings of Gandhi show the power that he thought there was in non-violent protest:

- Non-violence is more powerful than all the weapons in the world.
- In non-violence the masses have a weapon which lets a child, a woman, even an old man resist the strongest government successfully.

1 When a famous person dies, an article about him or her appears in the newspapers. It is called an obituary. It usually includes all the good things about the person. Write an obituary for Gandhi. Include what he did in South Africa, his love for the Untouchables and the fact that he helped them by non-violent protests.

2 If someone picks a fight with you, which is more difficult:
- to run away
- to fight back
- to stand up to them without fighting?
Talk with your partner about it.

3 Think of something that is wrong today. Suggest things you might do – like Gandhi – to protest about it without using violence.

Everyone knows what it means if there is one of these signs outside a house.

When people sell their house they may be moving nearby or far away. A move may mean a new job and a new school for the children. But most people stay in the same country.

When people decide to move to another country, everything is new and strange. They have to say goodbye to many of their friends and family. They may never see them again. They may have to get used to a different climate. The most difficult thing is when they have to learn a new language.

There are 500,000 Hindus living in Britain. Some came in the 1950s. Britain invited them to come. Britain needed help to rebuild the country after the Second World War.

Others came in the 1960s. They were forced to leave their homes in east Africa where their families had settled.

Often they use a room in a house for their temple. Or they buy a hall to use. Sometimes they build their own Hindu temples.

▶ *This is a Hindu temple in Leicester, England. Do you think this was built as a temple?*

◄ *Hindu teenagers in Western clothes*

Hindus have lived in Britain for many years now. Their children have been born here. They have grown up and had their own children here. They are British. Britain has always been made up of different races. There is no such thing as a British race. A British person is someone who is born here and sees Britain as their homeland.

Young Hindus enjoy Western fashions in clothes and music. But their families may want to keep their Indian backgrounds. This can cause problems. Some teenagers want more freedom than their parents allow:

- Some Hindu families want the women to wear saris at home.
- Teenage boys and girls may not be allowed to mix freely. They are not allowed to have sex before marriage.
- Some Hindu parents want an arranged marriage for their son or daughter.

There is no need for Hindus to choose either a Western or an Indian way of life. Young Asians are now mixing these together in many new ways. There are Asian DJs who have mixes that blend Indian styles of music with Western. Some Western groups also take on Indian influences.

1 a) Write a letter to an agony aunt about ONE difficulty a Hindu teenager might have.

b) Read out your letters in class. Talk about how you could reply.

c) Write a reply to your letter.

2 Ask your teacher to bring in some examples of Asian mixes to play, or to try to find Western music that has been influenced by Asian styles.

Glossary

ahimsa – non-violence
ancient – very old
arti – religious ceremony in which fire is offered to God
arranged marriage – when a marriage partner is chosen by the parents
Aum – a symbol for God

Bhagavad Gita – see *Gita*
Brahma – one of the 3 most important gods
Brahman – God as an impersonal force
Brahmin – a Hindu priest

caste – group into which you are born
caste system – Hindu class structure
ceremony – something which is done with set words and actions
conscience – our inner voice that tells us what is right and wrong
cremation – burning up of a dead body

dharma – a Hindu's duty according to their caste
dowry – gift given by the bride's parents

fast – to go without food
funeral pyre – a pile of wood on which a body is cremated

Ghandi – (Mahatma Gandhi), a great religious leader
Gita – the most popular Hindu holy book
guru – teacher

henna – red dye to decorate hands and feet
Hinduism – a religion
Hindu – a person who follows Hinduism
holy – set apart for God
horoscope – diagram of the stars and planets, used to tell people's fortunes

image – statue or picture of a god or goddess
incense – a tree gum or spice that is burnt to give off sweet smelling smoke
independence – freedom from government by another country

juggernaut – a very large lorry

karma – the law that every action has its effects
Krishna – one of the appearances of the god Vishnu

mandir – a Hindu temple
meditation – quiet thought
millennium – 1000 years
moksha – release from the endless circle of birth and death

non-violence – peaceful actions

pilgrim – someone who goes on a pilgrimage
pilgrimage – a religious journey to a holy place

Rama – one of the appearances of the god Vishnu
reincarnation – rebirth
religion – belief in God which affects how a person lives

sacred – holy
sacred thread – cotton thread given to wear when a Hindu boy comes of age
sadhu – a holy man
Sanskrit – language of the ancient Hindu holy books
sari – a length of cloth used as a woman's dress
sati – 'devoted wife', the practice in which a widow dies on her husband's funeral pyre
Shiva – one of the main Hindu gods
shrine – a place of worship with an image of a god
soul – the real you, the part of you that does not die
symbol – something that stands for something else
spiritual – the inner life

temple – a Hindu place of worship

Untouchables – Hindu outcastes

Vedas – the earliest Hindu holy books
vegetarian – someone who does not eat animals
Vishnu – one of the 3 main Hindu gods

yoga – a disciple of mind and body

Index